ISBN 978-1-334-45887-3
PIBN 10610025

1 MONTH OF
FREE
READING

at

www.ForgottenBooks.com

———◇———

By purchasing this book you are eligible for one month membership to ForgottenBooks.com, giving you unlimited access to our entire collection of over 1,000,000 titles via our web site and mobile apps.

To claim your free month visit:

www.forgottenbooks.com/free610025

English
Français
Deutsche
Italiano
Español
Português

www.forgottenbooks.com

Mythology Photography **Fiction**
Fishing Christianity **Art** Cooking
Essays Buddhism Freemasonry
Medicine **Biology** Music **Ancient**
Egypt Evolution Carpentry Physics
Dance Geology **Mathematics** Fitness
Shakespeare **Folklore** Yoga Marketing
Confidence Immortality Biographies
Poetry **Psychology** Witchcraft
Electronics Chemistry History **Law**
Accounting **Philosophy** Anthropology
Alchemy Drama Quantum Mechanics
Atheism Sexual Health **Ancient History**
Entrepreneurship Languages Sport
Paleontology Needlework Islam
Metaphysics Investment Archaeology
Parenting Statistics Criminology
Motivational

CONSTITUTIONAL

ASPECTS OF ANNEXATION

BY

CARMAN F. RANDOLPH

AUTHOR OF "THE LAW OF EMINENT DOMAIN"

[ADVANCE SHEETS OF THE HARVARD LAW REVIEW, JANUARY, 1899]

CAMBRIDGE
HARVARD LAW REVIEW
1898

CONSTITUTIONAL ASPECTS OF ANNEXATION.

Part First.

I.

WHETHER a European power shall indulge the appetite for land is a question merely of ability and expediency. An Englishman, a Frenchman, a Russian, or a German would not presume to discuss the right of his government to seize land anywhere, hold it by any tenure, and rule it at will. For these governments, however unlike in structure and purpose, enjoy alike sovereignty in its elementary form. What the government wills, that it may do without considering the act or its consequences in the light of an organic law of binding obligation. The Federal Government is in a different position. Its powers are conferred, and duties and restraints are imposed upon it, by a written constitution interpreted by an independent judiciary.

Whether the United States shall annex Spanish lands now in their military possession, or within the immediate sweep of their military arm, demands a more searching examination of the powers, the duties, the purposes of our republic as marked by the Constitution than has any question arising since the Civil War.

II.

The United States have the power of expansion. Chief Justice Marshall says: "The Constitution confers absolutely on the government of the Union the powers of making war and of making treaties; consequently that government possesses the power of acquiring territory either by conquest or by treaty."[1] A state may add to its domain by discovery and settlement, and the Supreme Court has recognized this method of acquisition as one approved by the law of nations;[2] though perhaps it may be approved more accurately as necessarily inferred from larger constitutional powers. Surely if a nation can buy or seize land it can find and keep land.

The power of expansion is illimitable in point of law. Whenever the President and Congress join in extending the sovereignty of the United States over a particular territory, their action must be respected by the courts without regard to its location. "Who is the sovereign de jure and de facto of a territory is not a judicial but a political question, the determination of which, by the legislative and executive departments of any government, conclusively binds the judges as well as all other officers, citizens, and subjects of that government. This principle has always been upheld by this court, and has been affirmed under a great variety of circumstances."[3]

Is the power to annex conditioned upon the formation of States out of the new territory? This question is not suggested by the acquisition of small tracts for specific governmental uses, such as coaling stations, or of vacant guano islands under the Act of 1856.[4] Nor can it be urged as a legal objection to annexation that the land in question is not to be annexed as a State, for the admission of a State is, like the selection of territory, a political matter beyond the competency of the courts. But, according to the spirit of the Constitution, the subjection of annexed territory to exclusive federal control is an abnormal and temporary stage necessarily preceding the normal and permanent condition of statehood. Chief Justice Marshall described the Territories as being "in a state of infancy advancing to manhood, looking forward to complete equality so soon as that state of manhood shall be attained."[5] Chief Justice Taney said that the power to admit new States

---

[1] American Ins. Co. v. Canter, 1 Peters, 511, 541.
[2] Jones v. United States, 137 U. S. 202, 212; Shively v. Bowlby, 152 U. S. 1, 50.
[3] Jones v. United States, 137 U. S. 202, 212.
[4] U. S. Revised Statutes, § 5570.
[5] Loughborough v. Blake, 5 Wheaton, 317, 324.

authorizes " the acquisition of territory not fit for admission at the time, but to be admitted as soon as its population and situation would entitle it to admission."[1]   And Justice Gray said: " Upon the acquisition of a Territory by the United States, whether by cession from one of the States, or by treaty with a foreign country, or by discovery and settlement, the same title and dominion passed to the United States, for the benefit of the whole people and in trust for the several States to be ultimately created out of the Territory."[2]

All the land ceded to the United States by the States was transferred upon the understanding that it should be formed into States eventually.   The Third Article of the Treaty of 1803, by which France ceded Louisiana, recites that " The inhabitants of the ceded territory shall be incorporated into the Union of the United States, and admitted as soon as possible, according to the principles of the Federal Constitution, to the enjoyment of all the rights, advantages and immunities of citizens of the United States. . . ." This article was construed by Chief Justice Marshall to mean " that Louisiana shall be admitted into the Union as soon as possible upon an equal footing with the other States ; "[3] and a like meaning is to be placed upon the Treaty of 1819, by which Spain ceded Florida, and the Treaties of 1848 and 1853, by which Mexico ceded California and New Mexico.   Thus, with the exception of Texas, which was annexed by force of the joint resolution admitting it as a State, the vast domain gained by the United States down to 1853 was acquired in trust for States to be subsequently admitted.

The promise of statehood was not expressed in annexing Alaska and Hawaii, and the bearing of this departure from custom upon a pending project of annexation will be noted later.

III.

There is some difference of opinion as to the precise source of the power of the United States to govern territory outside the limits of States.   Chief Justice Marshall said: " The power of governing and legislating for territory is the inevitable consequence of the right to hold territory.   Could this proposition be contested,

---

[1] Scott v. Sandford, 19 Howard, 393, 447.

[2] Shively v. Bowlby, 152 U. S. 1, 57.

[3] New Orleans v. De Armas, 9 Peters, 224, 235.

the Constitution of the United States declares that 'Congress shall have power to dispose of and make all needful rules and regulations respecting the territory or other property belonging to the United States.'"[1] And he said in a later opinion: "In the meantime Florida continues to be a Territory of the United States, governed by virtue of that clause in the Constitution which empowers Congress 'to make all needful rules and regulations respecting the territory or other property belonging to the United States.'"

"Perhaps the power of governing a territory belonging to the United States which has not by becoming a State acquired the means of self-government may result necessarily from the fact that it is not within the jurisdiction of any particular State, and is within the power and jurisdiction of the United States. The right to govern may be the inevitable consequence of the right to acquire territory."[2]

In Chief Justice Taney's opinion the power to "make all needful rules," etc., refers solely to land ceded by the States and the general power to govern territory "stands firmly" on the right to acquire it,[3] and this perhaps is the better because the simpler ground. But, to quote Chief Justice Marshall again, "Whatever may be the source from which the power is derived, the possession of it is unquestioned."[4] And it should be added that the scope of the power must be the same, whichever its source.

The States of the Union are under the jurisdiction of two legislatures, — Congress and the State legislature each has its appropriate sphere of authority. The Territories are under the exclusive control of Congress, whose position is defined in the following opinions of the Supreme Court: "By the Constitution, as is now well settled, the United States, having rightfully acquired the Territories, and being the only government which can impose laws upon them, have the entire dominion and sovereignty, national and municipal, federal and state, over all the Territories, so long as they remain in a territorial condition."[5] "Congress may not only abrogate laws of the territorial legislatures, but it may itself legislate directly for the local government. It may make a void

---

[1] Serè v. Pitot, 6 Cranch, 332, 336.
[2] American Ins. Co. v. Canter, 1 Peters, 511, 542.
[3] Scott v. Sandford, 19 Howard, 393, 432–444.
[4] American Ins. Co. v. Canter, 1 Peters, 511, 544.
[5] Shively v. Bowlby, 152 U. S. 1, 48.

act of the territorial legislature valid, and a valid act void. In other words, it has full and complete legislative authority over the people of the territories and all the departments of the territorial governments. It may do for the Territories what the people, under the Constitution of the United States, may do for the States." [1] Although the difference between federal and local affairs is not marked in the Territories by governments organically distinct, as in the States, it exists nevertheless, for Congress stands in a double relation to each Territory, caring for its local interests as a State government might, and treating it as a part of the republic in matters of federal concern.

IV.

May Congress exert its power over territory within its jurisdiction and outside the limits of States without regard to the Constitution?

A desire to possess new lands, coupled with a fear lest the extension of the Constitution to some of them at least and their people would both prejudice our own interests and hamper our rule, has begotten the proposition that annexed territory not admitted as a State is not an integral part of the " United States " and need not be governed by the law of the Constitution.

Although this proposition is suggested by an assumed emergency, it would, if established, affect equally all territory without the limits of States, — Alaska, Arizona, Hawaii, New Mexico, Oklahoma, and the District of Columbia would lie beyond the pale of the Constitution, and therefore under the arbitrary control of Congress.

The popular authority in support of the proposition is a passage in a recent opinion of the Circuit Court of Appeals for the Ninth Circuit sustaining an Act of Congress forbidding the importation, manufacture, and sale of liquor in Alaska. [2] The Court says: —

"In support of the first ground of demurrer, it is contended that the law upon which the prosecution is based is unconstitutional, because, among other things, the government of the United States can exercise only those specific powers conferred upon it by the Constitution ; that the Constitution guarantees to the citizens the right to own, hold, and acquire property, and makes no distinction as to the character of the property ; that intoxicating liquors are property, and are subjects of exchange, barter, and traffic like any other commodity in which a right of property exists ; that, inasmuch as the power to regulate commerce was

---

[1] National Bank v. County of Yankton, 101 U. S. 129, 133.

[2] Endleman v. United States, 57 U. S. App. 1, 86 Fed. Rep. 456, 458.

committed to Congress to relieve it from all restrictions, Congress cannot itself impose restrictions upon commerce by prohibiting the sale of a particular commodity; that if Congress has the power to regulate the sale of intoxicating liquors within the Territories as a police regulation, it can only enact laws applicable to all the Territories alike. The answer to these and other like objections urged in the brief of counsel for defendant is found in the now well-established doctrine that the Territories of the United States are entirely subject to the legislative authority of Congress. They are not organized under the Constitution, nor subject to its complex distribution of the powers of government as the organic law, but are the creation exclusively of the legislative department and subject to its supervision and control. Benner v. Porter, 9 How. 235, 242. The United States, having rightfully acquired the territory, and being the only government which can impose laws upon them, has the entire dominion and sovereignty, national and municipal, Federal and State. Insurance Co. v. Canter, 1 Pet. 511, 542; Cross v. Harrison, 16 How. 164, 193; National Bank v. Yankton Co., 101 U. S. 129, 133; Murphy v. Ramsey, 114 U. S. 15, 44; Mormon Church v. U. S., 136 U. S. 1, 42, 43; McAllister v. U. S. 141 U. S. 174, 181; Shively v. Bowlby, 152 U. S. 1, 48. Under this full and comprehensive authority, Congress has unquestionably the power to exclude intoxicating liquors from any or all of its Territories, or limit their sale under such regulations as it may prescribe. It may legislate in accordance with the special needs of each locality, and vary its regulations to meet the conditions and circumstances of the people. Whether the subject elsewhere would be a matter of local police regulation, or within State control under some other power, it is immaterial to consider. In a Territory all the functions of government are within the legislative jurisdiction of Congress, and may be exercised through a local government or directly by such legislation as we have now under consideration."

This passage is to be read as an affirmation of the unquestionably broad and exclusive power of Congress in administering the Territories, but not of a right to deal arbitrarily with persons and property therein, for it will be shown that the Supreme Court recognizes the Territories as part of the United States for most important purposes, and confirms to their people the great constitutional guarantees.

The words "United States" in the Constitution may be construed in some cases to refer to the States alone. For example, territorial courts are not technically courts of the "United States."[1] Pre-

---

[1] Benner v. Porter, 9 Howard, 242.

sumably, however, the "United States" is, in the language of Chief Justice Marshall, "the name given to our great republic, which is composed of States and Territories. The District of Columbia or the territory west of the Missouri is not less within the United States than Maryland or Pennsylvania," and, he added, "it is not less necessary, on the principles of our Constitution, that uniformity in the imposition of imposts, duties, and excises should be observed in the one, than in the other." [1]

The general and unqualified prohibitions imposed upon Congress are absolute denials of power without regard to place.

Said Chief Justice Taney in Scott *v.* Sandford : [2] —

"No one, we presume, will contend that Congress can make any law in a Territory respecting the establishment of religion, or the free exercise thereof, or abridging the freedom of speech or of the press, or the right of the people of the Territory peaceably to assemble, and to petition the Government for the redress of grievances.

"Nor can Congress deny to the people the right to keep and bear arms, nor the right to trial by jury, nor compel any one to be a witness against himself in a criminal proceeding.

"These powers, and others, in relation to rights of person, which it is not necessary here to enumerate, are, in express and positive terms, denied to the General Government ; and the rights of private property have been guarded with equal care. Thus the rights of property are united with the rights of person, and placed on the same ground by the Fifth Amendment to the Constitution, which provides that no person shall be deprived of life, liberty, and property, without due process of law. And an Act of Congress which deprives a citizen of the United States of his liberty or property, merely because he came himself or brought his property into a particular Territory of the United States, and who had committed no offence against the laws, could hardly be dignified with the name of due process of law.

"So, too, it will hardly be contended that Congress could by law quarter a soldier in a house in a Territory without the consent of the owner, in time of peace ; nor in time of war, but in a manner prescribed by law. Nor could they by law forfeit the property of a citizen in a Territory who was convicted of treason, for a longer period than the life of the person convicted ; nor take private property for public use without just compensation."

A quotation from the Dred Scott Case is apt to be discredited in many quarters because of resentment against the decision, but on

---

[1] Loughborough *v.* Blake, 5 Wheaton, 317.

[2] 19 Howard, 393, 450.

this point Justice Curtis concurred with the court in his dissenting opinion. He said of the power of Congress over Territories, " in common with all the other legislative powers, it finds limits in the express prohibitions on Congress not to do certain things ; that in the exercise of the legislative power Congress cannot pass an *ex post facto* law or bill of attainder, and so in respect to each of the other prohibitions contained in the Constitution " (p. 614). And he agreed further that property within the Territories was protected by the Fifth Amendment (p. 624). More restrained in expression, but equally to the point, is Justice Bradley's opinion : " Doubtless Congress, in legislating for the Territories would be subject to those fundamental limitations in favor of personal rights which are formulated in the Constitution and its amendments ; but these limitations would exist, rather by inference and the general spirit of the Constitution, from which Congress derives all its powers, than by any other express and direct application of its provisions." [1]

In another opinion of the Supreme Court we read, " Congress is supreme [over the Territories], and for the purposes of this department of its governmental authority has all the powers of the people of the United States except such as have been expressly or by implication reserved in the prohibitions of the Constitution." [2]

In Thompson v. Utah [3] it is held, " That the provisions of the Constitution of the United States relating to the right of trial by jury in suits at common law apply to the Territories of the United States is no longer an open question," [4] and further, " it is equally beyond question that the provisions of the National Constitution relating to trials by jury for crimes and to criminal prosecutions apply to the Territories of the United States." [5]

In Callan v. Wilson [6] a person convicted in the Police Court of the District of Columbia without the interposition of a jury was ordered to be discharged from custody, and the Court said (p. 550) : " There is nothing in the history of the Constitution or of the original amendments to justify the assertion that the people of the

---

[1] Mormon Church v. United States, 136 U. S. 1, 44.

[2] National Bank v. County of Yankton, 101 U. S. 129, 133.

[3] 170 U. S. 343, 346.

[4] See American Pub. Co. v. Fisher, 160 U. S. 464, 468 ; Springville v. Thomas, 166 U. S. 707.

[5] See also Reynolds v. United States, 98 U. S. 145, 154.

[6] 127 U. S. 540.

District may be lawfully deprived of the benefit of any of the constitutional guarantees of life, liberty, and property, especially of the right of trial by jury in criminal cases. . . . We cannot think that the people of the District have, in that regard, less rights than those accorded to the people of the Territories of the United States."

What is the status of the inhabitants of territory lying within the United States, but without the States?

The Constitution provides that "all persons born or naturalized in the United States, and subject to the jurisdiction thereof, are citizens of the United States and of the States wherein they reside." In the Slaughterhouse Cases [1] the Court said of this provision: "The distinction between citizenship of the United States and citizenship of a State is clearly recognized and established. Not only may a man be a citizen of the United States without being a citizen of a State, but an important element is necessary to convert the former into the latter. He must reside within the State to make him a citizen of it; but it is only necessary that he should be born or naturalized in the United States to be a citizen of the Union. It is quite clear then that there is a citizenship of the United States and a citizenship of a State, which are distinct from each other, and which depend upon different characteristics or circumstances in the individual."

In a recent opinion the Supreme Court said: "The Fourteenth Amendment affirms the ancient and fundamental rule of citizenship by birth within the territory, in the allegiance and under the protection of the country including all children here born of resident aliens, with the exceptions or qualifications (as old as the rule itself) of children of foreign sovereigns or their ministers, or born on foreign public ships or of enemies within and during a hostile occupation of part of our territory, and with the single additional exception of children of members of Indian tribes owing direct allegiance to their several tribes." [2]

We will consider next the status of persons residing within territory at the time of its annexation to the United States.

It is a rule of public law that a state by annexing territory becomes entitled to the allegiance of its people. In the words of Chief Justice Marshall, "The relations of the inhabitants with their for-

---

[1] 16 Wall. 36, 72. [2] United States v. Wong Kim Ark, 169 U. S. 649, 653.

mer sovereign are dissolved, and new relations are created between them and the government which has acquired their territory. The same act which transfers their territory transfers the allegiance of those who remain in it."[1] And the right to allegiance is quite as substantial where territory is annexed by conquest unconfirmed by treaty.[2]

There is no occasion for relaxing the rule when the identity of the ceding or conquered state is extinguished by the transfer of its entire territory. But when the land transferred is a part only of a national domain, a regard for the ties of nationality and a reluctance to claim an unwilling allegiance may lead the new sovereign to allow the inhabitants who wish to retain their old allegiance a suitable time within which they may settle their affairs and depart. This privilege of removal was accorded by the United States in the treaties by which they acquired Louisiana, Florida, California, and Alaska.

Are the inhabitants of the annexed territory whose allegiance is transferred to the United States citizens thereof?

The Sixth Article of the Treaty with Spain of 1819 reads: " The inhabitants of the territories which His Catholic Majesty cedes to the United States, by this treaty, shall be incorporated in the Union of the United States, as soon as may be consistent with the principles of the Federal Constitution, and admitted to the enjoyment of all the privileges, rights, and immunities of the citizens of the United States."

This Article as construed by Chief Justice Marshall " admits the inhabitants of Florida to the enjoyment of the privileges, rights, and immunities of the citizens of the United States."[3] And he added: " It is unnecessary to inquire whether this is not their condition independent of stipulation." This inquiry is now pertinent. Does not the citizen or subject of a foreign State whose allegiance has been transferred to the United States, by the transfer of the territory of his residence, become a citizen of the United States, whether the transfer be consummated by cession or by conquest? In other words, is not every person from whom the United States claims full allegiance a citizen? The Supreme Court has not been required to decide this question, but it seems that one owing full allegiance to the United States, and being

---

[1] American Ins. Co. v. Canter, 1 Peters, 511, 542.

[2] See Hall, International Law, § 206; Dana's Wheaton, page 435, note.

[3] American Ins. Co. v. Canter, 1 Peters, 511, 542.

therefore subject to all the duties and responsibilities of a citizen, should have a citizen's rights. There are now within the United States "citizens," "wards" (Indians), and "aliens." Is there room for "subjects" who will be burdened with duties without enjoying compensatory rights?

Citizens of the United States residing without the limits of States have not the constitutional right to be represented in Congress, which must nevertheless lay upon them the taxes required by the Constitution to be " uniform throughout the United States." Here is taxation without representation, — one of the major grievances of the American Colonies against Great Britain. In reply to the charge that the United States maintain a condition that the Colonies denounced, Chief Justice Marshall said: " The difference between requiring a continent with an immense population to submit to be taxed by a government having no common interest with it, separated from it by a vast ocean and associated with it by no common feelings; and permitting the representatives of the American people under the restrictions of our constitution to tax a part of the society which is either in a state of infancy advancing to manhood, looking forward to complete equality so soon as that state of manhood shall be attained, as is the case with the territories, or which has voluntarily relinquished the right of representation and has adopted the whole body of Congress for its legitimate government, as is the case with the District, is too obvious not to present itself to the minds of all." [1]

Not only are citizens not residing in States without a voice in federal affairs, they are without constitutional right to regulate their own. The entire sovereignty over territory outside of the States is vested in the Federal Government. This position has not been always conceded. It was questioned in the Dred Scott Case,[2] and Senator Douglas declared that the people of the Territories possessed sufficient "popular sovereignty" to decide for themselves whether slavery should exist within their respective communities. The doctrine of popular sovereignty in the Territories is incompatible with the fundamental conception of the Union of States, and is thoroughly discredited.[3]

---

[1] Loughborough v. Blake, 5 Wheaton, 317, 324.

[2] 19 Howard, 293; see especially Justice Campbell's opinion, page 501.

[3] See National Bank v. County of Yankton, 101 U. S. 129, 133; Murphy v. Ramsey, 114 U. S. 15, 44; Mormon Church v. United States, 136 U. S. 1, 44.

The right of Congress to govern the Territories is formally opposed to the principle that governments "receive their just powers from the consent of the governed," but it is justified by reasons like those by which, as we have seen, Marshall justified taxation without representation. Although Congress cannot surrender its supremacy, it usually concedes as large a measure of home rule to the Territories as is expedient. In the language of Chief Justice Chase, "The theory upon which the various governments for portions of the United States have been organized has ever been that of leaving to the inhabitants all the power of self-government consistent with the supremacy and supervision of national authority and with certain fundamental principles established by Congress."[1] Alaska is an exception to the rule because of its meagre population. Indeed, many years elapsed before Congress found it advisable to constitute it a "civil and judicial district."

Upon reviewing the opinions of the Supreme Court, it is confidently affirmed that the political control of all territory of the United States outside of the States is vested absolutely in Congress, which may prescribe any form of government and grant or withhold political privileges to the people at discretion. But it is affirmed with equal confidence, because upon the same authority, that these Americans possess the same personal and property rights that the people of the States enjoy. In the language of the Supreme Court: "The personal and civil rights of the inhabitants of the Territories are secured to them, as to other citizens, by the principles of constitutional liberty which restrain all the agencies of government, State and National; their political rights are franchises which they hold as privileges in the legislative discretion of the Congress of the United States."[2]

Bearing in mind the distinction between political privileges and personal rights, we may comprehend the effective meaning of two comments made by distinguished jurists upon the constitutional provision empowering Congress "to dispose of and make all needful rules and regulations respecting the territory or other property of the United States." Chancellor Kent said: "It would seem, from these various congressional regulations of the territories belonging to the United States [Territorial Regulation Acts] that Congress have supreme power in the government of them, depend-

---

[1] Clinton *v.* Englebrecht, 13 Wall. 434, 441.
[2] Murphy *v.* Ramsey, 114 U. S. 15, 44.

ing on the exercise of their sound discretion. That discretion has hitherto been exercised in wisdom and good faith, and with an anxious regard for the security of the rights and privileges of the inhabitants, as defined and declared in the ordinance of July, 1787, and in the Constitution of the United States. ' All admit,' said Chief Justice Marshall, ' the constitutionality of a territorial government.' But neither the District of Columbia, nor a territory, is a *state*, within the meaning of the Constitution, or entitled to claim the privileges secured to the members of the Union. This has been so adjudged by the Supreme Court. Nor will a writ of error or appeal lie from a territorial court to the Supreme Court, unless there be a special statute provision for the purpose. If, therefore, the government of the United States should carry into execution the project of colonizing the great valley of the Columbia or Oregon River, to the west of the Rocky Mountains, it would afford a subject of grave consideration, what would be the future civil and political destiny of that country. It would be a long time before it would be populous enough to be created into one or more independent states; and in the mean time, upon the doctrine taught by the acts of Congress, and even by the judicial decisions of the Supreme Court, the colonists would be in a state of the most complete subordination, and as dependent upon the will of Congress as the people of this country would have been upon the king and parliament of Great Britain, if they could have sustained their claim to bind us in all cases whatsoever. Such a state of absolute sovereignty on the one hand, and of absolute dependence on the other, is not congenial with the free and independent spirit of our native institutions; and the establishment of distant territorial governments, ruled according to will and pleasure, would have a very natural tendency, as all proconsular governments have had, to abuse and oppression."[1] And Judge Story said: " The power of Congress over the public territory is clearly exclusive and universal; and their legislation is subject to no control, but is absolute and unlimited, unless so far as it is affected by stipulations in the cessions, or by the ordinance of 1787, under which any part of it has been settled."[2]

If these comments have as broad a meaning as can be inferred from their texts, they are discredited by the opinions of the Supreme Court. But the suggestion that a bald despotism is

---

[1] Commentaries, i. 385.   [2] Commentaries, Section 1328.

possible in any part of the republic should not be imputed to the great commentators. Their comments should be considered together because Story's refers by a note to Kent's, and they may be construed to affirm simply the plenary power of Congress in the political administration of the Territories. Neither Kent nor Story can be fairly quoted as denying personal and civil rights to any of the American people. And we refer to these rights only when we assert that the general guarantees and prohibitions of the Constitution are as broad as the republic — not allowing to people living without the States any political franchise, any right of self-government, but assuring to them the rights of life, liberty, and property as they are defined by the Constitution.

PART SECOND.

The foregoing remarks on the constitutional aspects of annexation bear generally upon the several territorial questions growing out of the war with Spain, and especially upon the question of the Philippines.

I.

The United States are, as their name implies, a Union of States, and although in contemplation of law they may add to their domain without restriction as to place, each annexation should have for its object, be it near or remote, the creation of self-supporting and mutually supporting commonwealths. This conception of the republic as a union of States is consistent with the nationality of the American people, and it must be maintained if we are to contemplate free institutions throughout our land, for statehood is the single and conclusive mark of the ability of communities to govern themselves.

The United States, therefore, ought not to annex a country evidently and to all appearances irredeemably unfit for statehood because of the character of its people and where the climatic conditions forbid the hope that Americans will migrate to it in sufficient numbers to elevate its social conditions and ultimately justify its admission as a State. And when a project for annexing territory is coupled with a disclaimer of any intention of admitting it as a State now or hereafter, when this disclaimer is necessary in order to secure a favorable consideration, the project is opposed to the spirit of the Constitution.

The Philippine islanders are, and are likely to remain, unfit for statehood. Indeed, their inferior estate is admitted by the plea that we should embrace them because they are not fit even to govern themselves. Nor can we look forward to the peopling of the islands by Americans, for, whatever may be meant by the warning that " our frontiers are gone," and that we must provide land for " surplus population," the Philippines offer no inducements to American home-seekers. But it is argued that the Philippine project is in line with previous annexations which commit us to the proposition that statehood is not the necessary objective of annexed territory. This argument is worthless, and its illustrations are unimportant.

It is true that New Mexico and Arizona are not yet States, but the anticipation of statehood in which their domain was acquired will one day be realized. The purchase of Alaska was theoretically a deliberate departure from a sound rule, but it was in line with a policy approving the withdrawal of European sovereignty from America, and, after all, the republic is not actually prejudiced by holding a sparsely peopled territory that will probably become a veritable waste when the fur-bearing animals are exterminated and the gold is carried away. The acquisition of Hawaii was precipitated by the very war that has provoked the Philippine project to which it is too closely related to serve as a precedent, and, besides, the citizens in Hawaii may yet acquire a constitutional right of self-government by the incorporation of the islands with a Pacific State. As for the guano islet of Navassa, which appertains to the United States, we may decline to perceive a likeness between lighting on a vacant manure heap and seizing one of the greatest of archipelagoes.

II.

The disclaimer of any intention of carving new States out of the Philippines, whatever it may be worth, is not sufficient to render annexation palatable. It is supplemented by the announcement that the Constitution covers the States only, and that the Philippines can be ruled with a free hand.

A readiness to rule the Philippines arbitrarily is an unseemly feature of the annexation programme, not mitigated by the promise that justice and mercy will temper force. It will be recalled that a strong objection to the original Constitution was the lack of a Bill of Rights, and that the omission was rectified by the adoption of the first ten amendments. Can it be said that these amendments are superfluous or that the barriers we built for self-protection are not needed for the protection of Asiatics? Perhaps some of the amendments would be inappropriate in Asia, but we cannot pick and choose among them. Perhaps constitutional government in the Philippines would be a failure, but if Asiatics can be ruled only by a system which places their lives, liberties, and property at the disposition of the government, the work is unrepublican and not in our line.

I have shown that the opinions of the Supreme Court affirm the proposition that the Territories are within the purview of the Constitution, and this will be the position of the Philippines if they are annexed, for they cannot be acquired in a way that will differentiate them organically from our present possessions. The domain of our republic is divided into two primary classes only, — land subject to the jurisdiction of States and land not so subject. Congress may divide its possessions into political districts, but it cannot extend the Constitution to or withhold it from each district at pleasure. The Constitution is not at the disposition of Congress. It is superior to Congress. It is a self-extending law, and so far as it covers our present possessions must cover future ones. The proposition has an important bearing upon a commercial policy in respect of the islands and upon the status of the islanders.

It is asserted that having annexed the Philippines we would not be obliged to treat them as commercially a part of the United States, but could, for example, prescribe special customs regulations for them. Indeed, we hear the prediction that we would open the islands to the world's trade and help Great Britain open the door to China. So far as the assertion claims the support of law, it appears to rest upon the following passage from Chief Justice Taney's opinion in Fleming v. Page.[1] The Chief Justice after deciding that a port in the belligerent occupation of the United States is a foreign port in respect of our tariff laws said : —

" This construction of the revenue laws has been uniformly given by the administrative department of the government in every case that has come before it. And it has, indeed, been given in cases where there appears to have been stronger ground for regarding the place of shipment as a domestic port. For after Florida had been ceded to the United States, and the forces of the United States had taken possession of Pensacola, it was decided

---

[1] 9 Howard, 603, 616.

by the Treasury Department that goods imported from Pensacola before an Act of Congress was passed erecting it into a collection district, and authorizing the appointment of a collector, were liable to duty. That is, that although Florida had, by cession, actually become a part of the United States, and was in our possession, yet, under our revenue laws, its ports must be regarded as foreign until they were established as domestic by Act of Congress ; and it appears that this decision was sanctioned at the time by the Attorney-General of the United States, the law officer of the government. And although not so directly applicable to the case before us, yet the decisions of the Treasury Department in relation to Amelia Island, and certain ports in Louisiana, after that province had been ceded to the United States, were both made upon the same grounds. And in the latter case, after a custom-house had been established by law at New Orleans, the collector at that place was instructed to regard as foreign ports Baton Rouge and other settlements still in the possession of Spain, whether on the Mississippi, Iberville, or the sea-coast. The Department in no instance that we are aware of, since the establishment of the government, has ever recognized a place in a newly acquired country as a domestic port, from which the coasting trade might be carried on, unless it had been previously made so by Act of Congress.

" The principle thus adopted and acted upon by the executive department of the government has been sanctioned by the decisions in this court and the circuit courts whenever the question came before them. We do not propose to comment upon the different cases cited in the argument. It is sufficient to say that there is no discrepancy between them. And all of them, so far as they apply, maintain that under our revenue laws every port is regarded as a foreign one, unless the custom-house from which the vessel clears is within a collection district established by Act of Congress, and the officers granting the clearance exercise their functions under the authority and control of the laws of the United States."

Conceding the highest authority and the widest significance to this passage, it contemplates merely a transitory condition, — a period between the passing of an old régime and the complete establishment of a new one under the auspices of Congress, during which administrative authority is perforce supreme. In these circumstances the President may levy customs duties in the annexed territory, and we grant, for the sake of argument, that he may levy them at discretion. We will assume, for the sake of argument, that duties may be collected on goods brought hither from the new territory. But these actions are abnormal and provisional. They rest wholly upon the inaction of Congress. Of course Congress cannot be compelled to organize customs districts in new territory, and delay may be inevitable as, for example, when land is annexed at a special session of the Senate. Nor is Congress necessarily neglectful in extending tariff laws deliberately. But, making allowance for unimportant delays, it will appear that Congress is obliged by the letter and spirit of the Constitution to impose uniform duties within the political limits of the United States. They who would annex the Philippines in the hope that the islands will continue to be commercially separate from the United States prefigure a wilful and persistent neglect of duty on the part of Congress, and in consequence of this neglect the permanent regulation of Philippine customs by the President. Congress would not long permit the President to levy duties at his pleasure within territory subject to its proper jurisdiction.

Unless Chief Justice Marshall has erred profoundly, Congress could not adopt a customs policy peculiar to the Philippines, for in Loughborough v. Blake,[1] he said with regard to the declaration in the Constitution that "all duties, imposts, and excises shall be uniform throughout the United States," "The District of Columbia, or the territory west of the Missouri, is not less within the United States than Maryland or Pennsylvania; and it is not less necessary, on the principles of our Constitution, that uniformity in the imposition of imposts, duties, and excises, should be observed in the one, than in the other," and again (page 325), "The Constitution not only allows, but enjoins the government to extend the ordinary revenue system to this district" (of Columbia).

Loughborough v. Blake affirmed the power of Congress to levy a direct tax within the District of Columbia, but the opinion contains a masterly declaration of the great principle that all the territory within the jurisdiction of Congress is commercially one country.

Should the courts affirm that all persons owing full allegiance to the United States are citizens thereof, the annexation of the Philippines would naturalize collectively all islanders answering to this

---

[1] 5 Wheaton, 317.

description. Certainly all islanders born after annexation and within the allegiance of the United States would be citizens. (See case of Wong Kim Ark, *ante*, page 9.)

The opinion in the case of Wong Kim Ark [1] excepts from the rule of citizenship by birth Indians " owing direct allegiance to their several tribes." In Elk *v.* Wilkins [2] the Court said: " Indians born within the territorial limits of the United States, members of, and owing immediate allegiance to, one of the Indian tribes (an alien though dependent power), although in a geographical sense born in the United States, are no more ' born in the United States and subject to the jurisdiction thereof,' within the first section of the Fourteenth Amendment, than the children of subjects of any foreign government born within the domain of that government, or the children born within the United States of ambassadors or other public ministers of foreign nations." And it was decided in this case that an Indian does not become a citizen by living apart from his tribe, but can gain citizenship only through naturalization.

The segregation of tribal Indians from the body of the American people is an established feature of our polity. In the words of Justice Miller, " they always have been regarded as having a semi-independent position when they preserved their tribal relations; not as States, not as nations, not as possessed of the full attributes of sovereignty, but as a separate people, with the power of regulating their internal and social relations." [3]

If we should annex the Philippines, it may be assumed that we would classify as many of the islanders as possible under the head of " wards," " dependent nations, " or " tribal Indians." But this classification could not be made arbitrarily, for the constitutionality of our discrimination against the Indian is based on the fact that he owes allegiance to a political organization other than though inferior to the United States. Hence we could apply our Indian policy in the Philippines only to persons who have not been in fact within the jurisdiction of Spain, but have been governed by their tribal organizations.

After many of the islanders had been relegated to the condition of undesirable, troublesome, and expensive " wards," there would remain probably several millions whose claims to citizenship by

---

[1] 169 U. S. 649, 653. [2] 112 U. S. 94, 102.

[3] United States *v.* Kagama, 118 U. S. 371, 381.

allegiance might not be rejected, and whose children would be unquestionably citizens of the United States.

Among the rights incident to citizenship is that of moving freely throughout the length and breadth of the United States. Whether Malays would be induced to come here in sufficient numbers to lower the rate of wages in any part of the country, I do not discuss. But citizens have the right to compete with other citizens, and employers will go far for cheap labor.

Although citizens of the United States have not as such the right to vote, they may gain a residence in any State, and cannot be refused the suffrage therein on account of " race, color, or previous condition of servitude."

III.

May the United States assume permanent sovereignty over the Philippines without annexing them; that is to say, without making them a part of the republic? If this be lawful, our government may rule the islands unembarrassed by certain constitutional limitations and requirements that affect it within the United States, and inaugurate a provincial system capable of indefinite extension.

Although the question suggests a federal power over territory beyond the United States, the power itself must be derived from the Constitution.

The question cannot be answered by referring to the power to make treaties, for these are not extra-constitutional agreements. They are a part of the law of the land, and quite as subordinate to the Constitution as are acts of Congress, with which they rank in point of internal obligation.

The " general welfare " clause, that playground of lax constructionists, is ineffective, for it is " the general welfare of the United States," not the Philippines or Thibet or other outlying country. Equally ineffective is the power of Congress " to make all needful rules and regulations respecting the territory or other property of the United States," for whatever may be the precise meaning of this clause it contains no warrant for the ruling of provinces. The truth is that the territorial jurisdiction of Congress cannot be extended beyond the bounds of the republic for which only it is empowered to legislate and in which the Constitution is supreme.

There is but one constitutional power that affords an excuse for discussing the question, and that is the power exerted in declaring war, which gives the President a roving commission to invade and hold enemy country.

In Fleming v. Page,[1] the power to make war and the character of belligerent occupation were carefully considered. Chief Justice Taney said : " A war . . . declared by Congress can never be presumed to be waged for the purpose of conquest or the acquisition of territory ; nor does the law declaring the war imply an authority to the President to enlarge the limits of the United States by subjugating the enemy's country. The United States, it is true, may extend its boundaries by conquest or treaty, and may demand the cession of territory as the condition of peace, in order to indemnify its citizens for the injuries they have suffered, or to reimburse the government for the expenses of the war. But this can be done only by the treaty-making power or the legislative authority, and is not a part of the power conferred upon the President by the declaration of war. His duty and his power are purely military. As commander-in-chief, he is authorized to direct the movements of the naval and military forces placed by law at his command, and to employ them in the manner he may deem most effectual to harass and conquer and subdue the enemy. He may invade the hostile country and subject it to the sovereignty and authority of the United States. But his conquests do not enlarge the boundaries of this Union, nor extend the operation of our institutions and laws beyond the limits before assigned to them by the legislative power.

" It is true that, when Tampico had been captured, and the State of Tamaulipas subjugated, other nations were bound to regard the country, while our possession continued, as the territory of the United States, and to respect it as such. For, by the laws and usages of nations, conquest is a valid title, while the victor maintains the exclusive possession of the conquered country. The citizens of no other nation, therefore, had a right to enter it without the permission of the American authorities, nor to hold intercourse with its inhabitants, nor to trade with them. As regarded all other nations, it was a part of the United States, and belonged to them as exclusively as the territory included in our established boundaries.

" But yet it was not a part of this Union. For every nation which acquires territory by treaty or conquest holds it according to its own institutions and laws. And the relation in which the port of

---

[1] 9 Howard, 603, 614.

Tampico stood to the United States while it was occupied by their arms did not depend upon the laws of nations, but upon our own Constitution and acts of Congress. The power of the President under which Tampico and the State of Tamaulipas were conquered and held in subjection was simply that of a military commander prosecuting a war waged against a public enemy by the authority of his government. And the country from which these goods were imported was invaded and subdued, and occupied as the territory of a foreign hostile nation, as a portion of Mexico, and was held in possession in order to distress and harass the enemy. While it was occupied by our troops, they were in an enemy's country, and not in their own; the inhabitants were still foreigners and enemies, and owed to the United States nothing more than the submission and obedience, sometimes called temporary allegiance, which is due from a conquered enemy, when he surrenders to a force which he is unable to resist. But the boundaries of the United States, as they existed when war was declared against Mexico, were not extended by the conquest; nor could they be regulated by the varying incidents of war, and be enlarged or diminished as the armies on either side advanced or retreated. They remained unchanged. And every place which was out of the limits of the United States, as previously established by the political authorities of the government, was still foreign; nor did our laws extend over it."

A provisional control assumed by the President during a belligerent occupation may last until the end of the war, and if the territory does not then revert to its former sovereign, may be prolonged until a normal government shall be established.

This provisional control may continue by the sufferance of Congress after the territory has been annexed to the United States. For example, Congress never organized a government for California, but permitted the government instituted by the President during our hostile occupation to continue after the cession of the territory and until the State of California was admitted. The Supreme Court said in this relation: —

" The government of which Colonel Mason was the executive had its origin in the lawful exercise of a belligerent right over a conquered territory. It had been instituted during the war by the command of the President of the United States. It was the government when the territory was ceded as a conquest, and it did not cease as a matter of course or as a necessary consequence of the restoration of peace. The President might have dissolved it by withdrawing the army and navy officers who administered it, but he did not do so. Congress could have put an end to it, but that was not done. The right inference from the inaction of both is that it was meant to be continued until it was legislatively changed. No presumption of a contrary intention can be made."[1] It should be noted that whatever may have been the position of California during the belligerent period of the provisional government, the country became a part of the United States upon its annexation and was thenceforth within the purview of the Constitution.

There is but one way to rule the Philippines without annexing them, and that is by the authority of the President. In case the United States do not annex the islands by treaty their forces will nevertheless remain in possession after the passing of Spanish sovereignty. Our possession will be exclusive against the world. Internationally the Phillippines will be United States territory, but something will remain to be done before they become domesticated — Congress must legislate for them. When this is done the country will be a part of the United States because it has come under their normal sovereignty. Until this is done the President will hold and control the islands in the absence of obstructive legislation by Congress. In these circumstances he may withdraw the forces and leave the country to its fate; recognize a local government; make a disposition of the islands by diplomatic arrangement or, with the consent of the Senate, by treaty ; or continue his rule. He will be the arbiter of the Philippines by virtue of a possession begun under the authority of Congress and continued by its sufferance. In describing his powers as despotic I do not mean that they would be exerted with unnecessary severity, but simply that they would not be restrained by any law to which the islanders might appeal. (Whether, or how far Congress could guide the President's action in the Philippines by legislation directed to him or his American subordinates I do not discuss). Here is provincial government and it may last during the forbearance of Congress. Such a government is only reconcilable with the principles of the Constitution as a temporary arrangement made advisable by the results of war.

———————

We cannot extricate ourselves from the Philippine entanglement with credit by simply withdrawing our forces. Our operations in

———————

[1] Cross *v*. Harrison, 16 Howard, 164, 193.

Luzon have given the *coup de grâce* to the old order without perfecting a new one, and while we are not called upon to insure the peace of the islands, we are morally persuaded to exert our influence towards bettering their condition.

If the difficulties in the way seem to be insurmountable, it is only because they lie in a field of international action, in which, fortunately, we have not had much experience. Hitherto the United States have displayed little concern in the " control, disposition, and government " of foreign territory, though they have proclaimed and enforced the Monroe doctrine for the protection of American States. But the European Powers have made the minding of other people's business a matter of unremitting attention and frequent experiment. Many of their actions in this regard are forbidden to us by constitutional or moral considerations ; none perhaps would serve as a model for our precise imitation ; but they suggest that there is an opportunity to do justice to the Philippines and promote our commercial interests in the East without annexing the islands or ruling them as provinces in derogation of our republican principles.

I am sufficiently impressed with the power of my country in regard to the Philippines to believe that any disposition of them that it would be likely to commend would be tolerated if not approved by the Maritime Powers. Nor would their toleration be due alone to respect for the United States. I think that in our eyes the Philippines are magnified beyond their true proportions on the political map of the world. Rich as these islands may be, important as is their strategic position, the aggressive Powers are pre-empting or seizing richer lands and better vantage-grounds with no more serious consequences as yet than " strained relations " or " demonstrations."

An acceptable solution of the Philippine problem might be achieved by pursuing one of the following courses : —

I. Neutralize the Philippines and recognize a local government. Accord recognition upon conditions that will afford due protection to foreign interests, including perhaps the institution of an international court, as in Egypt, and foreign supervision of the customs, as in China, or even of fiscal matters generally, as in Egypt.

II. Neutralize the Philippines and either establish a government on somewhat the same lines as the Congo Free State, or transfer them to an unobtrusive but competent state, like Holland.

III. Recognize the titular sovereignty of Spain over the islands, but transfer their entire administration to another Power. Such is the situation of Cyprus and Bosnia, which, nominally Turkish, are fully governed by Great Britain and Austria respectively.

IV. Transfer the Philippines to any Power that can be reasonably expected to rule them wisely and humanely and open them to the world.

These courses do not exhaust the possibilities but rather suggest them ; and a practicable disposition of the Philippines other than their annexation to the United States will reward a determined effort to accomplish it.

Upon the assumption that the pending Treaty of Paris provides for the cession of the Philippines, it is asserted that we are so deeply committed to annexation that further opposition would be unbecoming, if not unpatriotic. This assertion belittles the greatest of all the powers especially confided to the Senate. There is a courteous presumption in favor of a treaty presented to the Senate, but nothing more. A treaty of peace that cannot be amended by the Senate without danger of reopening hostilities has of course a peculiar claim to ratification. The Treaty of Paris is not in this category. Nor is it a document chiefly of international concern intended to promote the renewal of friendly relations between the United States and Spain. Assuming that the annexation of the Philippines is embodied in the treaty, it is the most questionable project of domestic concern that a President has ever submitted to the Senate.

MORRISTOWN, NEW JERSEY, *December 11*, 1898.

CPSIA information can be obtained
at www.ICGtesting.com
Printed in the USA
BVHW042249140219
540160BV00056B/1938/P

9 781334 458873